Someone you know has committed suicide. You are facing a very hard, dark reality. You feel rocked, hurt, betrayed, and confused. You are experiencing a whole range of emotions and reactions. Each one is painful. Your initial reaction was probably shock and disbelief. Now you are trying to make sense of what happened. How do you come to terms with the suicide of someone you know? Can you make any sense out of such a senseless act? Can you find hope in the aftermath of such a desperate choice? How does knowing God make a difference as you grieve?

What You Are Facing

You are experiencing a storm of emotions and feelings. First, you are feeling the natural response of deep grief. Someone you know and love has died. So you feel the emptiness and sorrow of loss. That alone is extremely hard. But suicide adds many other painful reactions to the heartache that death brings. The death was self-inflicted. You are probably also experiencing one or more of these emotions:

- *Confusion and disorientation.* What happened *is* confusing and disorienting. Suicide is never neat and tidy. Most likely you are still struggling to accept the reality of this tragedy.
- *Anger and betrayal.* By definition, suicide cuts other people off. So you may experience feelings of anger and a sense of betrayal.
- *Guilt and responsibility.* It's normal to wonder, *Could I have done something?* Or, *If only I'd done _____.* Or, *Why didn't I notice _____?*
- *Fear of doing the same thing.* Someone else's suicide might make you fearful that you could do the same thing. You might be afraid that you also are at risk for suicidal behavior.

You are facing unanswerable questions. Everyone who is touched by suicide wrestles with "Why? Why did this happen? Why did it have to come to this? Why couldn't it be stopped?" But no matter what reasons there were for the suicide, in the end, it can never be completely explained. You are left with questions

Grieving a Suicide

Help for the Aftershock

David Powlison

New
Growth
Press

www.newgrowthpress.com

New Growth Press, Greensboro, NC 27429
Copyright © 2010 by Christian Counseling & Educational Foundation
All rights reserved. Published 2010.

Cover Design: Tandem Creative, Tom Temple, tandemcreative.net
Typesetting: Robin Black, www.blackbirdcreative.biz

ISBN-10: 1-935273-68-X
ISBN-13: 978-1-935273-68-4

Library of Congress Cataloging-in-Publication Data

Powlison, David, 1949-
    Grieving a suicide : help for the aftershock / David Powlison.
        p. cm.
    Includes bibliographical references.
    ISBN-13: 978-1-935273-68-4 (alk. paper)
    ISBN-10: 1-935273-68-X (alk. paper)
    1. Suicide—Religious aspects—Christianity. 2. Bereavement—Religious aspects—Christianity. 3. Grief—Religious aspects—Christianity. I. Title.
    BV4905.3.P69 2010
    248.8'66—dc22

                                              2010023087

Printed in Canada.

17 16 15 14 13 12 11 10   1 2 3 4 5

FSC
Mixed Sources
Cert no. SW-COC-000952
© 1996 FSC

that can't be answered because the person who committed suicide is gone. (For help in understanding the reasons for suicidal thoughts and actions, see, *I Just Want to Die: Replacing Suicidal Thoughts with Hope*[1]).

Facing a Suicide by Faith

How can you deal with this painful experience? There is no quick and easy solution to what you are facing. And God, in the Bible, doesn't offer you platitudes and pat answers. He gives you something much better—in response to your sorrow, your emotions, and your unanswered questions, he gives you himself.

Edith Schaeffer once used a tapestry metaphor to talk about the difficult things in life. She pointed out that the front of the tapestry was a beautiful pattern, but the back was a mass of knots and tangled threads. Your loved one's suicide is one of the tangled and knotted areas on the back of your tapestry. No matter how long you look at it, you won't be able to make sense out of it. This is one of life's broken, dark experiences in which you must find that the promises and presence of your God and Savior are real. In the midst of this grave darkness, God calls you to live a life where faith and love still shine.

One day, you will see the front side of the tapestry, instead of just the tangled back. One part of the beauty of the tapestry will be the way you learn to know God and love others by going through difficult experiences. Is that the whole answer to why God let it happen? No. There are things about his will and his purposes that are beyond us. The Bible says, "The secret things belong to the LORD our God, but the things revealed belong to us and to our children forever, that we may follow all the words of this law" (Deuteronomy 29:29).

The reasons for the suicide of the one you love are among "the secret things" that belong to the Lord. But "the things revealed belong to us and to our children forever." God isn't only talking about his laws; he's also talking about his promises, his purposes, his revelation of himself in Jesus and the Word. What has been revealed is given so you can live. What hasn't been revealed to you is meant to be a secret thing. Instead of trusting in your knowledge, you have to trust in God's love and goodness. This is a lesson you will have to learn and relearn all through your life—not only now as you struggle with this heartache, but through all the ups and downs that life brings. Your relationship with God will be what brings you peace, not having all of your questions answered.

You will never have an answer that ties up all the loose ends. You will never feel good about it. You won't "get over it" in the sense that it won't hurt or trouble you anymore. You will live with an ongoing sense of "I don't understand. It's still not right, every time I remember." The suicide of someone you love brings great, ongoing weakness into your life.

C. S. Lewis captured this condition of our comprehensive weakness. He said that our need for God is revealed in our "growing awareness that our whole being by its very nature is one vast need, incomplete, preparatory, empty yet cluttered, crying out for him who can untie things that are now knotted together and tie up things that are still dangling loose."[2] Experiencing the suicide of someone you love will put you in a place where all you can do is rely on God, the only one who can untie the things that are knotted together and tie up things that are dangling loose.

You have to say, along with the apostle Peter, "Lord, to whom shall we go? You have the words of eternal life. We believe and know that you are the Holy One of God" (John 6:68–69). Where else will you go? Who is bigger than the things in your heart that are tied in knots or dangling loose? After all the struggling to make sense, after all the sickening grief at the finality of the act, after all the anger at the betrayal, at a fundamental level you must be able to say, "I do not understand this and I must leave it with you, my God and my King."

Faith Grows in Weakness

God is not naïve to the realities that drive someone to suicide. Nor is he naïve to your struggle with grief and pain. It is right in the middle of these hard realities that your faith and trust in God grows. God explains it this way:

> "Blessed is the man who trusts in the
> LORD, whose confidence is in him. He will be
> like a tree planted by the water that sends out
> its roots by the stream. It does not fear when
> heat comes; its leaves are always green. It has no
> worries in a year of drought and never fails to
> bear fruit." (Jeremiah 17:7–8)

Jeremiah is talking about living in a desert where life is hard and brutal. The desert in the Bible is the place of death. There's no water, no food. It's hot. There are dangerous predators and poisonous snakes. It is the place where your faith is tested. Do you feel that your grief and confusion have brought you into a spiritual desert? As you deepen your trust in God, your desert will become the place where you find God's living water of hope, mercy, and blessing.

God's living water is his presence. He says, "I am with you." He is the only person who can profoundly reassure your heart. Though you are feeling alone and abandoned, he is with you. His presence means that even in the darkest of circumstances (including the suicide of someone you love) you can be unafraid. Let me say it again.

> *He* is with you.
> He *is* with you.
> He is *with* you.
> He is with *you*.

Because God is with you, you will be fruitful, even in the aftermath of heartache and perplexity.

No "magic wand" can make the memory of your loved one's suicide not hurt. You must remind yourself many times that the eternal God is with you, and he is bigger than death. He promises that one day death will be ended, and all sorrow, pain, and tears will be wiped away (Revelation 21:4).

Practical Strategies for Change

The actions of those around us influence us both for good and bad. You might say that we counsel each other with our actions. When someone you love commits suicide, you are receiving some very bad counsel. The counsel that comes from a suicide is that the way to deal with disappointment and hardship is to isolate oneself. Suicide is an act done in isolation that leads to utter isolation and desolation. You need to resist this counsel by clinging to God, by connecting with other people, by trusting in God's mercy, and by living in a way that is fruitful.

Cling to Jesus

The first thing you must do is take refuge in the God who promises his steadfast love. Taking refuge in him means facing the dark reality of suicide, but not staying stuck in all of your negative reactions—the "why" questions, the sense of abandonment, or even thinking that suicide is a viable way to deal with your pain. The way out of these bad reactions is to find someone who is bigger than what has happened. And that someone can only be the Lord of life, your Savior, Jesus Christ.

Suicide brings suffering and difficulty into the lives of everyone who is touched by it. But God has come, in the person of Jesus, and entered into the difficulties, the sufferings, the sins, and the disappointments of this life. Jesus bore your weakness. He was tempted as you are. He triumphed. Now he comes near to you with promises of mercy and goodness. "He who did not spare his own Son, but gave him up for us all—how will he not also, along with him, graciously give us all things?"(Romans 8:32).

As you read through Romans 8, you notice that Paul doesn't say that we won't have hardships. Instead he acknowledges that there will be "trouble...hardship...

persecution…famine…nakedness [and] danger" (v. 35). But he *does* promise that none of these things "will be able to separate us from the love of God that is in Christ Jesus our Lord" (v. 39). Cling to this promise. Cling to Jesus. Invite him into your struggles, your sorrows, and your questions. Fill your mind with his words.

When you read the Gospel of Luke, you read a very unusual biography of Jesus. Luke doesn't talk much about famous, smart, successful people. He focuses on little people, people who are powerless, bereaved, ignored, and neglected. Right now you are there. You're going through something far bigger than your ability to control or fix. As you read Luke, watch Jesus in action. Notice how he treats people with wisdom, love, and tenderness. Notice how he's content to do and say only one thing, or a few things. Take to heart that this is also the way he treats you.

As you read through the Psalms, take them and pour out your heart to Jesus. The Psalms will give you patterns for how to bring your particular troubles to Jesus, your Savior and Friend. Ask him to be with you through this time. He promises to answer when you call (Psalm 86:7). He promises to never leave you or forsake you (Hebrews 13:5).

Connect with People

Another thing you must do is connect honestly with others. Don't try to handle this apart from your community. Gather with those who also have been affected by the suicide. Talk with each other about your loved one. Don't avoid talking about the suicide. Being together at the funeral and afterwards will bind you to one another in shared sorrow. This coming together to grieve and remember is the opposite of the message of isolation and aloneness that suicide speaks.

The tragedy of suicide doesn't have to tear relationships apart. Family can pull together more tightly, and friendships can become deeper as you cling to each other in the face of life's difficulties. Don't try to go down the dark path of life's tough realities without joining with others. These relationships will always remind you of the empty chair—the person who's not with you. But genuine human community is one of God's greatest gifts. Your community can help you fight against the isolation, despair, and implicit hostility that are part of a suicidal act. Pray with and for each other as you grieve.

Trust in God's Mercy

One question that may be lurking in your mind is, "Can my loved one still go to heaven after committing suicide?" This is a natural question for a Christian to ask. Suicide is wrong. It's self-murder, and that is a sin. But it is important to remember that it's not the unpardonable sin. We don't read hearts. We don't know the whole story. We don't know what went on between your loved one and God in her final moments. You can't climb back into her last moments and know what she was thinking about. But you do know for sure that God is just, merciful, and forgiving. And you also know that you can't presume to know God's inner mind and purposes.

If your loved one had faith in Christ, even though her last act on earth was wrong, that doesn't mean she can't be forgiven. God knows hearts—we don't; and he, who is both just and merciful, makes the final decision about heaven and hell.

You need to be willing to live with something less than 100 percent closure about the answer to this question. "The secret things belong to the LORD our God" (Deuteronomy 29:29). You can only do this as you are certain of God's love. Ponder Romans 8, concentrating especially on verses 31–39. They are full of the promise of God's mercy, his presence in Jesus Christ, and the love of God that is unquenchable and indestructible. Fill your mind and heart with the promise of God's love, and you will be able to trust him with your loved one's life.

Live Fruitfully

It's important at this time that you don't neglect the basics of life. Your food might not have much taste, but you need to eat. You may not feel like getting out of bed in the morning, but you need to get up and get dressed. You might have little interest in your work or household responsibilities, but you need to keep going. Take time to grieve, to process…and get back to normal living. Doing these things makes the statement that life continues despite what has happened.

As you live in community with God and with others, and reestablish normal living patterns, you will notice over time that you have the ability to love other people more consistently and deeply. Paul, in his second letter to the Corinthian church, said that God "comforts us in all our troubles, so that we can comfort those in any trouble with the comfort we ourselves have received from God" (2 Corinthians 1:4).

Nothing will bring your friend, relative, or coworker back. But you can become a wiser friend, more willing to take a risk and step in when you see something that's hard. God will use what you are going through now to give you wisdom and tenderness as you reach out to others who are suffering. God's comfort will flow through you so that you can comfort others in their trouble.

Your loved one chose, in his or her last act on earth, to live destructively. In response to that, it is important to ask God to help you live fruitfully. Living fruitfully means taking refuge in God, loving others, and "running the race" the whole way through. It means living each day knowing that your life belongs to Jesus and, because of that, continuing to take small steps forward even when life is overwhelming. As you do this, you are facing the darkness that suicide brings and responding by living in the light and hope of the gospel of Jesus Christ.

Endnotes

1 David Powlison, *I Just Want to Die: Replacing Suicidal Thoughts with Hope* (Greensboro, NC: New Growth Press, 2010).
2 Lewis, C.S., *The Four Loves* (New York: Harcourt, Brace, 1960), p. 3.

Simple, Quick, Biblical

Advice on Complicated Counseling Issues
for Pastors, Counselors, and Individuals

MINIBOOK
CATEGORIES

- Singles
- Marriage & Family
- Medical & Psychiatric Issues
- Personal Change

E YOURSELF | GIVE TO A FRIEND | DISPLAY IN YOUR CHURCH OR MINISTRY